OUR NEW CLOTHES: ACQUISITIONS OF THE 1990s

OUR NEW CLOTHES: ACQUISITIONS OF THE 1990s

Richard Martin

Photographs by Karin L. Willis

The Metropolitan Museum of Art, New York
Distributed by Harry N. Abrams, Inc., New York

This volume has been published in conjunction with the exhibition "Our New Clothes: Acquisitions of the 1990s," held at The Metropolitan Museum of Art from April 6 through August 22, 1999.

The exhibition is made possible by B A R N E Y S   N E W Y O R K

Published by The Metropolitan Museum of Art, New York

John P. O'Neill, Editor in Chief
Barbara Cavaliere, Editor
Design by Matsumoto Incorporated, New York
Barbara Cavaliere, Production

Library of Congress Cataloging-in-Publication Data:

Martin, Richard (Richard Harrison)
    Our new clothes : acquisitions of the 1990s / Richard Martin
            p.   cm.
    Catalog of an exhibition held at The Metropolitan Museum of Art, New York, N.Y., Apr. 6-Aug. 22, 1999.
        ISBN 0-87099-900-1 (alk. paper). —
        ISBN 0-8109-6540-2 (Abrams : alk. paper)
        1. Costume—Exhibitions. 2. Costume Institute (New York, N.Y.)—Exhibitions. I. Metropolitan Museum of Art (New York, N.Y.) II. Title.
    NK4709.M38   1999
    746.9'2'0747471—dc21   99-14145
                                            CIP

The color photography in this volume is by Karin L. Willis, The Photograph Studio, The Metropolitan Museum of Art.

All the costumes and library materials in this volume are in the collection of The Costume Institute, The Metropolitan Museum of Art.

Color separations by Professional Graphics, Rockford, Illinois
Printed by Julio Soto Impresor, S.A., Madrid
Bound by Encuadernación Ramos, Madrid
Printing and binding coordinated by Ediciones El Viso, Madrid

Front cover: French, *Man's ensemble (coat with alternating cuffs, and waistcoat)* (detail), ca. 1765. See overall view on page 42.

Back cover: Drécoll, *Robe en Pannier dress*, 1912. See overall view on page 17 and another detail on page 8.

CONTENTS

FOREWORD

With this exhibition, we are entering an unusual period in The Costume Institute. Ever since Richard Martin arrived, it was clear that exhibitions would be born of his own fertile mind and not in response to outside suggestions—not even mine. Richard is a most determined fellow. It was thus with some trepidation that, following a conversation with curator Gary Tinterow, I raised the possibility of a collateral costume exhibition for this fall's exhibition of paintings and drawings "Portraits by Ingres: Image of an Epoch." In reply, Richard first put forward, in high rhetoric, a justification of the prized curatorial autonomy of his department and the strides The Costume Institute had made in exhibition, interpretation, and research. Then Richard, smiling broadly, indicated that, these things having been achieved, it was now a perfect time for a collaborative effort.

Although I was flush from this victory, it was still with some hesitancy that, when Richard mentioned a cancelled exhibition, I indicated it would be nice if The Costume Institute would, one day, like some other curatorial departments, show recent acquisitions. This time Richard's answer was immediate and uncharacteristically laconic: "Fine, we'll do it this spring." But, *quod erat expectandum*, it was also clear that the exhibition would not be treated as an illustrated inventory but be given a definite context through a suite of vignettes composed of acquisitions limited to the past decade.

I am pleased that two of my suggestions for 1999 exhibitions in The Costume Institute have been accepted. I further acknowledge that "Our New Clothes" is such an astounding exhibition because of the many generous donors to The Costume Institute who understand that fashion as a living art confers a special responsibility on any institution that professes to address and collect costume and fashion. We must keep up with this living art of our time. We must provide a richer, deeper knowledge of the past, and we must concomitantly build a collection for the future.

It is especially satisfying to note that this emphasis on collecting has occurred with no sacrifice in research or exhibition quality and quantity. Indeed, Richard Martin has already organized nineteen exhibitions—almost all deeply rooted in our collection—since his tenure began in 1993.

I am most grateful to Barneys New York for its generous sponsorship of "Our New Clothes."

Richard Martin is fond of saying that The Metropolitan Museum of Art has become a major fashion collector without being a fashion victim. For my part, I am pleased to acknowledge the many wearers, makers, and collectors who have helped both the cause of The Metropolitan Museum of Art and the possibilities in costume research, interpretation, and exposition by giving so generously to The Costume Institute. Their old clothes have become our new clothes. We shan't wear them, but we will keep them with the covenant of an institution that is nothing less than the world's finest collection of costume, intent upon continuing to be that and more, thanks to old and new clothes and to our commitment to render or keep them new through ideas, research, and exhibition.

Philippe de Montebello
Director
The Metropolitan Museum of Art

A HISTORY OF FASHION

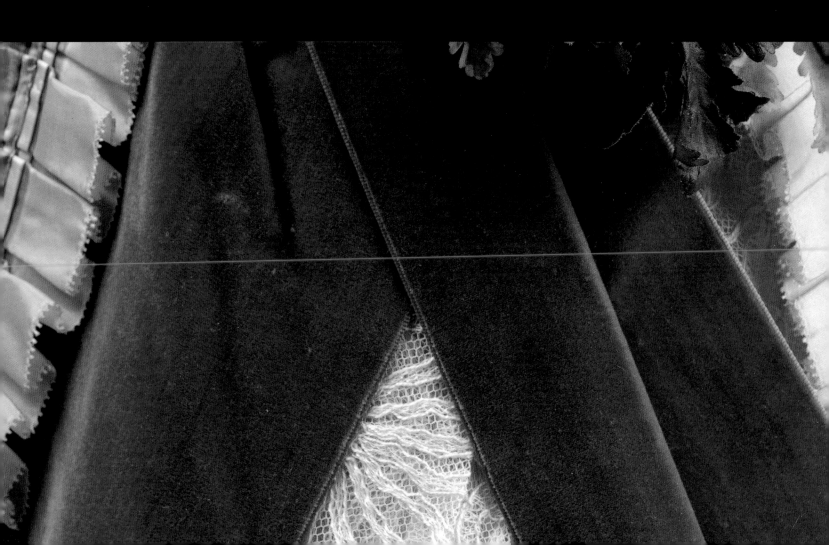

Unequivocally stated, "A History of Fashion" sounds like the responsibility of a learned lifetime or the title of a prodigious tome, certainly not the gatherings of a decade. But it is evident here that, in the past ten years, we have collected the equivalent of a solid survey of the history of Western dress from 1700 to the present. Landmark pieces are found where, despite the extraordinary fact that they could stand on their own as a fine collection of costume, they provide resonance to the peerless collection assembled over fifty-five years. Like the great orchestra, a collection is composed of independent greats; one just would not have expected the full orchestra so amplified in strength in so recent a time period.

Purchases have been especially strong in the eighteenth century, a sentimental favorite of all costume historians in part because it is costume's first extensively documented era, the longest historical view through extant objects. Moreover, the objects remain arrestingly beautiful. It could seem a miracle that an eighteenth-century mantua is still in excellent condition.

We are now very selective in acquiring eighteenth-century dress. The collection sets a high standard: we can acquire better, but there is no point in selecting anything inferior to what we already have. Thus, the English robe à la française (pp. 12-13) was selected as a prime example of its kind. With all elements complete, including delicate nettings and floss, and in an extremely fine state of preservation, it can serve as a textbook example. Yet, the ivory damask robe à la française (shown herein) is irresistible because it is an elegant puzzle, like a Malevich white-on-white painting in a rococo frame. It is always important to remember to learn from objects, not textbooks, for this is a museum, not a reading room. (One is especially aware of this simple truth in a credulous field such as costume history.)

We know that we are not likely to receive as gifts from individual donors clothing dating prior to 1912. The rule of thumb I use is that individuals are willing to donate clothing if they remember a mother or grandmother wearing it. Beyond that memory, all is history. No sweet madeleine of remembrance will reach it.

We carefully put our modest acquisitions funds into critical exhibition-worthy pieces that will strengthen our collection overall. Work on exhibitions demonstrates the collection's strengths and weaknesses. Exhibitions often shake the trees. Clothes trees. Madame Grès donations were prompted by the exhibition devoted to the designer; the "American Ingenuity" show prompted questions such as, "I have American designer dresses. I just didn't know you were interested. Are you?"

Before an addendum of accessories, we end this chapter with a Versace dress that was inspired by the Metropolitan Museum's own exhibition "The Glory of Byzantium" (1997). The designer, who was a habitual visitor to the Museum, applied Byzantine crosses in his fall 1997 couture collection, as shown in June 1997, days before his murder. That December, this dress was shown in the exhibition "Gianni Versace." In such an instance, one is aware that ours is no mere echelon of objects but a museum's extraordinary capacity to offer history for potential contribution to a creative future. All that we possess is a treasure for us and even more for the future.

English

Mantua and petticoat (front and back
views), 1708
"Bizarre" salmon-pink silk damask brocaded
with polychrome silk floss and gold metallic filé
and frisé thread
Purchase, Rogers Fund, Isabel Shults Fund,
and Irene Lewisohn Bequest, 1991
(1991.6.1a-c)

By 1708, the mantua, previously a form of
undress, was high style and ripe for its own
secession to the robe à la française as the
commanding style of formal dress for the
eighteenth century. This rare example,
unaltered and intact with ruffles, advances
the century's interest in bold textile, often
more to the scale of home furnishings than
dress, though the swag of its bustle makes
it still transitional.

English

Robe à la française (open robe and petticoat)
(and detail of sleeve), 1740s
Hand-painted cream silk moiré faille,
crocheted netting, cream silk fly-fringe,
and polychrome flowers of silk floss
Purchase, Harris Brisbane Dick Fund, 1995
(1995.235a,b)

A perfect example of the robe à la française
at mid-century, this hand-painted silk dress
displays the opulence, Orientalism, and
insatiable baroque excess of the time. Layers
build on layers; flowers terrace out from the
two-dimensional on the textile, to silk flowers,
to nets laden with trapped flowers and floss.
A Chia-dress for the eighteenth century, its
sleeves are braceleted with more flowers.
The silhouette is perfectly of the era: panniers
dilate the hips; a narrow waist is achieved by
the corset, which further pushes up and
supports the bust. A deep décolletage is
rendered more or less modest with insertions
of bits of cloth, and the sleeves are finished
with layers of engageants that are generally
just basted in for easy detachment and
washing and are thereby useful in keeping
the valued dress clean.

American

Robe à l'anglaise (round gown), ca. 1775
Emerald-green silk damask
Purchase, Irene Lewisohn Trust Fund, 1994
(1994.406a-c)

This dress is considerably less gaudy than
continental and English clothing of the period.
Yet, it is not lacking in sumptuousness. Rather,
the green Spitalfields damask, attributed to
Anna Maria Garthwaite about 1743-45, is richly
displayed. The Costume Institute acquired this
dress in 1994, knowing that it would be in the
Museum's exhibition "John Singleton Copley's
America." It has since appeared in our show
"The Ceaseless Century." One could argue that
the relative simplicity engenders more delight in
the dress's inherent voluptuousness.
Generations later, it was said that Boston ladies
waited a year before breaking out their new
Paris finery from Worth; perhaps the American
sensibility in luxury goods is slow and
deliberate. The outfit includes matching shoes.

French (?)

Dress (open robe, petticoat, and fichu),
ca. 1798
Fine Indian mull embroidered with
polychrome silk thread
Purchase, Irene Lewisohn and Alice
L. Crowley Bequests, 1992 (1992.119.1a-c)

The French Revolution changed dress.
Court styles were abandoned; most clothing
was cotton and could seem to be only the
chemise or undergarment of the styles a
generation earlier. The political idealism was
democracy. The vestige of the *ancien régime*
is found in the open robe as indebted to the
robe à la française, but in such simplified and
softened form as to be barely recognizable.

English

Robe à la française (open robe, petticoat, and stomacher), ca. 1760
Canary-yellow silk taffeta
Purchase, Arlene Cooper Fund and Polaire Weissman Bequest Fund, 1996
(1996.374a-c)

Monochrome, but in a bright canary yellow guaranteed to catch anyone's attention across a room, this exceptionally well-preserved robe à la française with trimmings represents the apogee of the form. The absence of ornament, other than basic ruffles, makes this a museum object easy to read: it is a perfect teaching example, free from distractions and affirming thereby the adorned beauty of eighteenth-century silhouette and style, so often masked under frills and coquetry.

French

Pierrot bodice, ca. 1785
Warp-printed striped silk/linen blend of cream, yellow, pink, and green
Purchase, Davenport/Fleisher, Irene Lewisohn, and Isabel Shults Funds, 1998 (1998.253.1)

Differentiated from the full-fledged Pierrot costume, the Pierrot as a shaped bodice flourished in that last gasp of rococo sensibility and extreme silhouette of about 1780 to 1790. The flared peplum extension of the jacket below the waist asymmetrically around the back allows for the bulbous, billowing skirt of the period. The self-fabric ruffles on the bodice make it almost a condensed version of the open robe of that period and slightly earlier.

American or European

Dress (top: day bodice, bottom: evening bodice), ca. 1855
Ivory organza printed with green and black rose pattern
Gift of James R. Creel IV and Mr. and Mrs. Lawrence Creel, 1992 (1992.31.2a-c)

The middle of the nineteenth century possesses a special depth of imagination, ranging from Honoré de Balzac to Queen Victoria to Scarlett O'Hara, and this dress would disappoint not a one of them. Equipped with two interchangeable bodices, one for day and one for evening, it might seem to anticipate career dressing or, even more interestingly, women becoming practical about fashion. Less practical are the splendid tiers of organza in wedding-cake-like circular layers. Research in the Woodman Thompson collection of Dated Fashion Plates confirms the suspected date; the country of origin is considerably more difficult because, with the popularity and proliferation of fashion plates, ideas and textiles were carried fast and far.

Agnès Drécoll

Robe en Pannier dress (and details on page 8
and back cover), 1912
Yellow silk taffeta with blue and cream stripes,
blue velvet, cream embroidered net,
and silk flowers
Purchase, Davenport/Fleisher, Irene Lewisohn,
and Isabel Shults Funds, 1998 (1998.253.3)

This sumptuous dress, in which an Edwardian
silhouette emerges from an S-curve, is one
of our best examples of eighteenth-century
revival and was acquired for its first showing
in our fall 1998 exhibition "The Ceaseless
Century." Its robe à la polonaise silhouette,
open robe format with petticoat revealed at
center front, deep décolletage, ruching with
pinked edges, and laces are conspicuous
eighteenth-century revival themes. The dress
is unabashedly modern yet also harks back
"ceaselessly into the past," as the early
modern inexorably does.

American

Young boy's suit (habit dégagé), ca. 1810
Brown cotton and muslin with thin red stripes
Purchase, Judith and Ira Sommer Gift, 1997
(1997.509a-d)

Small in scale, rich as documentation, this
boy's suit in the New Republic double-
breasted, cutaway style with trousers (not
breeches) and with cream muslin jabot echoes
the male style for new citizens.

Jean Patou

Evening dress (and detail), ca. 1925
Tan silk velvet embroidered with polychrome
silk thread and gold and green beads trimmed
with gold lace
Purchase, Gifts from various donors, 1994
(1994.145)

In silhouette nothing more than T-shirt
dressing, this Patou evening dress assumes
the new aesthetic of dress as cylinder and
ornament as a glamorous light sheen on a flat
surface. Orientalist flowers and the delicate
palette emphasize the affinity to Callot Soeurs.
Patou is an important designer; The Costume
Institute has also recently acquired a 1920s
sports ensemble we attribute to him and used
in the winter 1998-99 exhibition "Cubism
and Fashion," there calling attention to his
propensity to the flat plane and Cubist form.

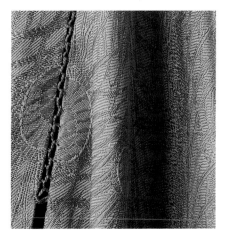

Liberty & Co.

Cape (and detail), 1900-1910
Pink and green silk Jacquard weave
Purchase, Isabel Shults Gift Fund, 1995
(1995.5.2)

The convergence of dress reform and
exuberance for travel unfolding like a new
map in Europe and England at the turn of the
century provided the world of Liberty & Co.,
rich in innovation, gentle in wrapping,
extravagant in color, and exotic in every luxury
of the senses. Fabric manufacturer and
London store, Liberty came to stand for the
cosmopolitan in such fashion as this evening
cape with gentle drape that suggests
Pre-Raphaelite painting and anticipates the
designs of Fortuny and Gallenga.

Agnès Drécoll

Evening ensemble (bolero and dress)
(and detail), ca. 1936
Orange silk crêpe embroidered
with silk floss and metal-wrapped thread
and blue-gray wool crêpe
Gift of Miss Julia P. Wightman, 1990
(1990.104.11a–c)

Displaying a Chinoiserie delicately appropriated
from the decorative arts, Drécoll's coral-orange
bolero is worn atop her Western-style
(but cheongsam- or qi-pao-related) column
dress. The result is a Shanghai-like synthesis
of East and West. By the 1930s, the frequent
trade expositions in Paris had encouraged keen
awareness of Chinese costume and arts
among French fashion designers, including
Grès, Lanvin, and Drécoll. Drécoll cleverly
used the exoticism of the bolero to set the
rank badges onto Western dress as a kind of
acknowledged appliqué.

Madame Grès

Evening ensemble (bodice and skirt)
(and detail), early 1980s
Navy/rose changeant silk rib weave,
rose/navy changeant silk rib weave
and dark-blue silk shantung
Gift of Mary M. and William W. Wilson, III,
1996 (1996.128.1a,b)

The story that Madame Grès first wanted to
be a sculptor could well have begun with
this dress. Its wonder is in its self-confident
shape. In this instance, the donor gave us a
critical piece of information that one could only
obtain from someone who had worn the
dress. The bubble skirt is the bottom of the
tunic, fitting over the skirt. The donor would
stuff tissue paper into the skirt in order to
achieve the desired fullness. Major gifts of
Grès pieces have enhanced the collection,
especially since our fall 1994 Grès exhibition.
Leading donors have included Mrs. Ahmet
Ertegun and Chessy Rayner.

Madame Grès

Evening gown (front and back views),
late 1960s-early 1970s
Orange silk jersey
Gift of Mrs. J. Gordon Douglas, Jr., 1996
(1996.448.2)

Grès had the capacity to seemingly drape the
dress before our eyes; here she navigated
the figure with loose tangerine silk jersey.
Creating a fusion of caftan (a favorite form of
hers) and dress, Grès scooped deep in the
back and skimmed along a neckline, letting a
ruffle extend over both arms, all this over a
straight skirt. A tour de force of dressmaking,
this example adds to the richest holdings of
Grès clothing anywhere.

Mainbocher

Evening ensemble (bolero and dress),
late 1950s
Apricot cotton net embroidered
with gold-tone sequins and beads
Gift of C. Z. Guest, 1999

Vogue (April 1, 1959) commented: "In fact,
Mainbocher, with his lifelong, often repeated
aim of 'simplifying fashion,' might have
been divinely appointed to be Mrs. Guest's
dressmaker—or Mrs. Guest, with her passion
for simplicity, to be his customer." Guest's
exquisite understated taste is legendary;
she found her fashion match in the refined
American sensibility of Mainbocher.

Gianni Versace

Evening dress, fall-winter 1997-1998
Gold-tone metal mesh with cross appliqué
Gift of Gianni Versace, 1999

Byzantine mosaics and gold, chiefly through
the forms of Ravenna, were a recurrent design
fascination for Versace, beginning with
fall-winter 1991-1992. For fall 1997, which he
did not live to see, he had designed gold-mesh
(a Versace signature) and leather dresses with
Byzantine crosses inspired by having seen
"The Glory of Byzantium" exhibition at The
Metropolitan Museum of Art. Thus a museum
shows art and inspires art; interprets history
and becomes a part of the historical process.

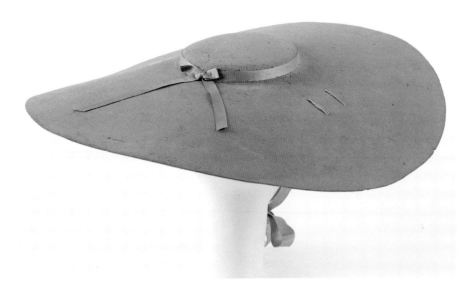

European (probably German)

Hat, 1720-1750
Brown felt and brown silk satin
Purchase, Isaac Fletcher Fund by Exchange
and Irene Lewisohn Charitable Trust, 1998
(1998.230)

This cartwheel hat of the eighteenth century
is an incredible find in good condition. It seems
a miracle that it has survived to serve, as it did,
in a comparison with a twentieth-century
cartwheel hat of the 1940s in our 1998
exhibition "The Ceaseless Century."

American or European

Bonnet, 1820-1835
Embossed paper and cream silk
Purchase, Judith and Gerson Leiber Fund,
1996 (1996.267)

Paper is the theme. What could have been
a straw bonnet is instead made of paper.

English

Hat, ca. 1760-1770
Embossed paper trimmed with black
and white silk floss
Purchase, Gift from various donors, 1997
(1997.369)

A rare, quite flat hat would have perched
precariously atop the head; embossed paper
was used instead of fabric.

American

Handbag, ca. 1860
Plaited newspaper lined in red silk twill with
red ribbon bows at the handles
Gift of Richard Martin, 1996 (1996.386.1)

Plaited newspaper was used for this handbag
and not because of a dearth of fabric (given
the lining). Could it have been motivated by a
desire for media coverage, newspaper as
a sign of modernity?

Isabel Canovas

Pump, fall 1988

Hot-pink silk satin embroidered with black
chenille and sequin ants

Gift of Richard Martin, 1993 (1993.34)

A hint of Dali-Schiaparelli-like Surrealism or
at least of mischief resides in these pumps.

Byron Lars

Shoe, spring 1994

White kid leather, black leather and wood

Gift of Byron Lars, 1997 (1997.246c,d)

Lars's elevated shoe invokes the geta
(Japanese wooden clog) or chopine (a high-
soled sixteenth-seventeenth century shoe).

THE WHITE DRESS

If this selection of "The White Dress" captures one tenth of the ardor of John Singer Sargent's paintings of women in white, then it succeeds magnificently. What Adam Gopnik has affectionately called "Sargent's Pearls" (*The New Yorker*, 15 February 1999) describes the impalpable snowy beauties of that painter. We showcase similar beauties in this chapter.

We probably feel that we know the virginal and radiant whiteness of many of these dresses, but our first example confronts us with an enigma in ivory. The eighteenth-century robe à la francaise (see p. 30) must have seemed a strangely chalky presence in the middle of an era in a ballroom or court obsessed with intense color, polychromatic dress, and decoration. We are drawn to this dress though, as certainly as to any of the other white dresses in this grouping, by its confident abstemiousness, its denial of color. Moreover, we are surely also fascinated by its watermelon-striped inner lining. Do we not feel in some way about this wondrous dress as we do about the coy, clinging dresses that grace page 39. Is the coy reserve of a 1998 Gucci gown so different from our fascination with her coquettish counterpart. After all, is white bashful or bold?

We offer a sweet promenade of delicate white dresses that pose some of the toughest questions about the history of fashion. Body definitions vary from Empire slackness to the exaggerated corseted waist of the 1830s. Tiers of sheer material billow about a severe silhouette with flirtatious softening, creating a penumbra at its radiant snowy core. White linen—the dishcloth kind, very temptingly tactile—in an eighteenth-century dress is a palpable field for applied ornament, whereas sparkling embroidery becomes the dress in the Armani version. The sparkle that almost blinds in a Hollywood dress by Ralph Lauren continues the tradition of what had begun in a linen robe à la polonaise centuries before and possibly then for the stage.

All these ladies may be dressed in white, but no two are the same. They all have wonderfully distinct character. The nineteenth-century bridal gown made in a distinctly dix-huitième style indicates a bride (or her parents) determined to live out of her time, expressing her yearnings for an earlier epoch.

Another ingenue shimmers with the excitement and glamor of Hollywood; it is hard not to imagine this dress generating optimism and romance. Other longings prevail for the contemporary designs. A nonchalant classicism, the happenstance of seeming like Madame Grès but more clearly for the beach and for the moderns (though Grès was often for both), is necessary for Demeulemeester to offer a drapery *à l'ancienne* but without a strained and tawdry post-modernism. Tom Ford for Gucci strives to skim as lightly over Halston as the fabric skims over the body, and John Galliano takes care to select from Vionnet without letting a 1920s-inspired dress fall into the trap of seeming "old-ladyish." Surely, if white is the new, it is of the old as well.

Women in white have haunted the romantic imagination for centuries. Through their diversity mingled with discipline, so clearly desisting color as a worldly essential, they have haunted the fashion imagination as well.

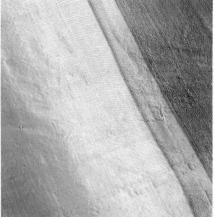

French

Robe à la française (and details), ca. 1770
Ivory silk damask
Funds from various donors, (1999.41 a, b)

Into the dazzling rococo kaleidoscope of 1770s
dress, someone had the bold idea to cast
an ivory dress. Is this utmost austerity and/or
the dress of the wallflower at the party?
Or is this dress that special chic that is
practiced in disregard of all the mandates and
an audacious, attention-getting dress?
The wearer's own secret is the watermelon
lining (second detail above), apparently a textile
that has been recycled, a common practice
for eighteenth-century linings. One of our
newest acquisitions, she (the dress, but surely
we know "her") is a wondrous mystery,
soliciting our research and imagination.

English

Robe à la Polonaise (robe and petticoat)
(and details), ca. 1780
Cream linen with polychrome chintz appliqué,
gold embroidery, and metal sequins
Funds from various donors, 1998 (1998.314a,b)

The element of eighteenth-century dress
that we probably think of first is court style.
That this linen dress has beauty, simplicity,
provincialism, and even a degree of vulgarity,
is most instructive. The bodice and skirt
sewn together constitute a robe; a matching
petticoat is worn underneath. Heavy linen,
almost of diaper weight and of great tactility,
will always feel luxurious, but with a common
touch. Likewise, the floral appliqué is clumsy
and garish, rather oversized for the dress.
But this country cousin possesses her own
charm, and the dressmaking is sure.

English

Round gown, ca. 1798

White cotton with polychrome crewel embroidery

Funds from various donors, 1998 (1998.222.1)

The exemplary silhouette, excellent condition, and delicate wool crewel embroidery of this round gown mark it as a stunning document of the late eighteenth century, when elements of classicism, such as the use of lightweight cotton textiles, foreshadowed the neoclassical style of the First Empire. Of course, the round gown still bears some remembrance of the open robe of the eighteenth century, even as crisp forms give way to a new fluidity and softness.

American

Dress, 1790s

Pink taffeta with fine stripes of cream silk and
metallic thread brocaded with metallic sprigs
Purchase, Coby Foundation Fund, 1998
(1998.269)

The fullest merger of old and new is
represented in this dress. The form of the
surrounding robe is open, and even the
neckline could seem to be decades earlier.
But the textile design has been subdued, and
the lighter taffeta robe is paired with a white
petticoat for an effect that resembles
neoclassicism emerging from the chrysalis
of the *ancien régime*.

American

Dress, ca. 1840

White cotton
Gift of Richard Martin and Harold Koda
in Honor of Cora Ginsburg, 1993 (1993.32)

The extravagant silhouette of this day dress
with bishop sleeves and pointed boned
waist demonstrates the evolution from the
nearly amorphous first cotton dresses of the
century to the grandest crinoline-supported
crystal palaces of the 1860s. It is a dress fit
for a heroine in a novel by one of the Brontë
sisters—shaped, expressive, tempestuous,
and beguiling.

American or European

Dress (and detail on page 28), 1830s

White cotton

Gift of James R. Creel IV and Mr. and
Mrs. Lawrence Creel, 1992 (1992.31.5)

With its high waist, leg o' mutton sleeves,
and swelling bell-shaped tiered skirt with
embroidered trim at tiers as well as cuff and
neck, this 1830s dress demonstrates the
gentle dilations of the silhouette that occurred
during the nineteenth-century and that
pumped and shaped the body in variable
directions and forms, filling out the repertoire
of trims and adornments.

American

Day dress, ca. 1880

White cotton

Purchase, Irene Lewisohn Trust, 1993
(1993.42a,b)

While among the most prized pieces of
historical clothing and occasionally seen in
vintage clothing sales, the cotton dresses
of the 1880s are seldom preserved in fine
condition, as they were made of a fine
batiste cotton. Further, they must often
have become elements of family theatricals
("the grandmother") and enactments early
in this century, many becoming altered
and abused in the process. This fine day
dress with a trained bustle skirt could be
a textbook example.

American

Wedding dress in the style of eighteenth-century robe à la française, early 1880s
Ivory ribbed silk damask and ivory ribbed silk with overlay of embroidered cream chiffon
Gift of Richard Martin, 1998 (1998.271a,b)

Like the day dress shown at the bottom of page 34, this wedding gown is of eighteenth-century revival style and indicates the intense interest during the 1880s in a return to the *ancien régime*. Notable elements of the revival style are: robe à la française silhouette with an extended Watteau back, rich oversized damask print, ruching at center front, eighteenth-century décolletage with lace fringe, and sleeves tapering into faux-engageants. Every bride wants something old; this one clearly wanted the old century. When we showed this gown in our 1998 exhibition "The Ceaseless Century" in the gallery called "The Masked Ball," it created a highly effective allusion to the eighteenth century.

American

Dress (and detail), ca. 1902-1904
White cotton mull trimmed
with white cotton lace
Gift of Mrs. Oscar de la Renta, 1994
(1994.192.18a-c)

The apogee of the summer white cotton dress
is evident in an example such as this one.
Canted with a monobosom to the swanlike
S-curve of the time, the dress is an ethereal
froth of white cotton mull with tucked mull and
lace trim with a tulip train. By the harsh times
of World War I, such dresses vanished entirely,
as did the tranquil golden age that produced
them and that is embodied in their serenely
cool gentleness and involution. One could think
of such as a *Brideshead* dress.

It was with this dress in mind
(I remember the dress from her lovely
presence in the summer garden party in the
1997 exhibition "The Four Seasons") that I
wanted to do a gallery of white dresses in
"Our New Clothes." She is too demure to be
a John Singer Sargent-like painted pearl but
rather is a gem of her own kind.

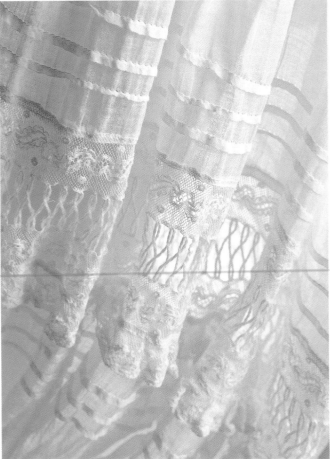

Giorgio Armani

Evening dress, fall-winter 1994
White silk embroidered with white silk thread,
white and silver-tone beads and sequins
Gift of Giorgio Armani, 1997 (1997.247.3)

By demanding simplicity of design,
Armani allowed for the possibilities of
a monochromatic opulence of texture played
off against the reserved silhouette.
Design seems contracted, but the dress
remains a symphony in white, playing on
every texture and resonance of whiteness.

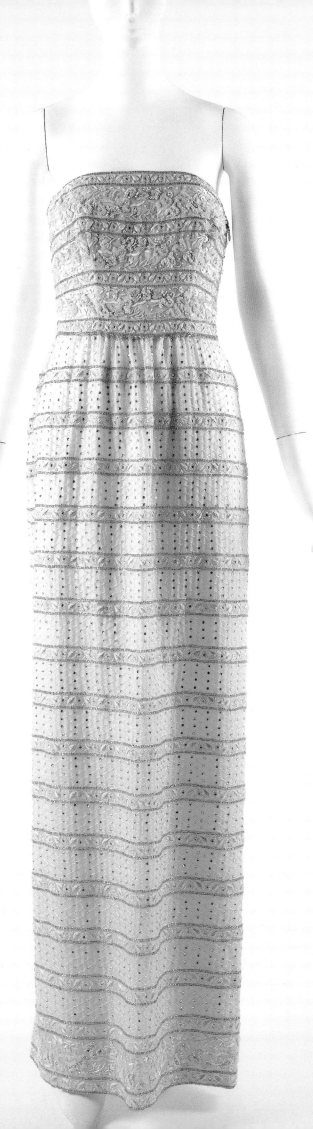

Ann Demeulemeester

Dress, spring-summer 1997
White Rayon
Gift of Richard Martin, 1997 (1997.456.1)

A tank dress or simple Rayon column bears
little inherent form, but it becomes a caryatid
by means of an interior fabric tape that hitches
to the waist. High fashion has long understood
such internal mooring, most notably
exemplified by Balenciaga's swaying baby-doll
silhouettes. Here, a simple, easy summer
white dress resembles a supple, provisional
version of Madeleine Vionnet or Madame Grès.

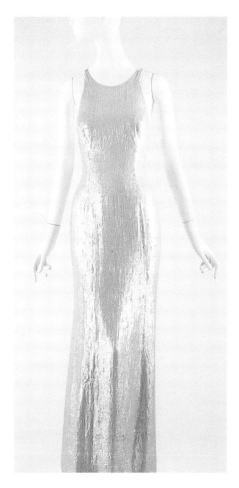

Ralph Lauren

Evening dress, spring 1995

White silk embroidered with white sequins

Gift of Ralph Lauren, 1999

The Hollywood dress by Lauren is an essay in simplicity. In monochromatic white, it offers pure light and undistracted attention to the body; it is sure to divert attention from anyone else on screen or at the gala. It is a perfect "entrance dress," one that can refract the lights of flashbulbs right back at the paparazzi.

Tom Ford for Gucci

Evening dress with belt, 1998

White silk jersey and brass

Gift of Gucci, 1999

Tom Ford designed, with more than a nod to Halston, this slinky silk jersey in a far less constructed version of Vionnet. Like all the dresses on this page, it suggests the strong influence of the 1930s, first of Paris initiatives and then of Hollywood versions.

John Galliano

Evening gown, spring-summer 1994

White silk jersey

Gift of Richard Martin, 1995 (1995.433.2)

This floor-length sheath is composed of two diagonally seamed rectangles and a horizontal rectangular panel around the bodice. For inspiration, Galliano has gone directly to Paris and Vionnet. Like China, the First Empire, and the Edwardian era, Vionnet is a recurrent source for Galliano: the Vionnet and 1930s influence was also profoundly present in his spring-summer 1989 collection. Among the Vionnet notes seen here are the cowl neckline and the petal-shaped ties in gray and black chiffon and white jersey at the right shoulder.

MEN OF THREE CENTURIES

Men are often forgotten in costume collections. Old menswear is often recycled into womenswear. Men tend to wear out their clothing. Men tend to vest less ostensible interest in their clothes and think it unworthy to donate to collections. As a result, there has been a dearth of exhibitions with equal or greater interest in menswear, and few collections are strong enough in menswear holdings to sustain such an exhibition. (Exceptions include Ann Coleman's "Of Men Only: Men's and Boys' Fashions, 1750-1975" exhibition, ill-served by its brochure, at the Brooklyn Museum, 1975-76; and Richard Martin and Harold Koda's exhibition, though limited to the twentieth century and better served by its book, *Jocks and Nerds*, at the Fashion Institute of Technology, 1989.) In 1990, The Costume Institute displayed many menswear items in the exhibition "The Age of Napoleon," but few were from our collection. Virtually all the pieces in our 1996 "Two by Two," in which men and women were always in tandem, were, however, drawn from our collection. In order to create that show, we selected the menswear pieces first, drawing upon the smaller variety; we then found escorts among our womenswear pieces. It would have been impossible, given the disproportion of the womenswear collection, to work in the opposite direction. Our predecessors mounted an ambitious "Adam in the Looking Glass" exhibition in 1950, combining a historical survey from the collection with commissioned designs from contemporary designers for future menswear.

Yet The Costume Institute's menswear collection, the above notwithstanding, is astonishingly strong. The chief deterrent to a menswear show is lack of mannequins. But we have been wheedled, cajoled, and even coerced to such a strength in menswear, in part by the relationship we enjoy with the NAMSB (National Association of Men's and Boys' Sportswear Buyers) Foundation. For very nearly the entire decade, the NAMSB Foundation has made an annual financial contribution to The Costume Institute expressly to support the acquisition of menswear.

Another good friend to the collection is Cora Ginsburg. One of her first gifts to celebrate the arrival of Harold Koda and me at the Museum, delivered wrapped only in two tattered pieces of tissue on her visiting the 1993 "Infra-Apparel" exhibition, and at first glance looking like old napkins from a yard sale, is the extraordinary pleated man's eighteenth-century shirt on page 42.

In view of the twentieth-century menswear selected for this book, it may be necessary to affirm that we have some conventional menswear of the era in our collection. (We also have some wonderful twentieth-century dandies among earlier donations, from the Duke of Windsor and Cecil Beaton, for instance.) Even those men are hardly seditionaries: a Gaultier jacket articulates the form of the nude body front and back, creating an image of invisibility; Rei Kawakubo for Comme des Garçons deconstructs the man's business suit, an easy target for some mockery even as viable as it continues to prove to be; a sailor's middy blouse goes from the starched white of the good sailor to the leather black of the more sinister sailor; and peacock flair reemerges in the 1990s. These may not be for the man on the street, but they make it a pleasure to be a boulevardier.

French

Man's ensemble (coat with alternating cuffs, and waistcoat) (and detail on page 40 and the front cover), ca. 1765
Peach silk velvet and pale-green silk satin embroidered with polychrome silk and metallic thread and green and gold sequins
Purchase, Isabel Shults Fund, 1994
(1994.405.1a,b,e,f)

This splendid coat comes with detachable cuffs with embroidery matching that of the waistcoat. Perhaps a practical element, as it doubles the use of the ensemble, the feature of removable cuffs betokens the abiding interest of menswear in the small details. Even today, features such as French cuffs or barrel sleeves are defining in menswear.

American

Man's shirt, late 18th century
Cream linen
Gift of Cora Ginsburg, 1993 (1993.142.1)

A shirt for the hero of *Tom Jones*, this linen origami of pleated shirting suggests the attention afforded to a gentleman's linens in the eighteenth century. The flare, or self-cravat, suggests the peacock that such a man was. This piece is a real rarity; there is one similar shirt in the collection of Colonial Williamsburg in Virginia.

English

Man's suit, ca. 1760

Purple wool with gold-bullion braid trim

Purchase, NAMSB Foundation Inc. Gift, 1996

(1996.117a-c)

This exceptional suit, not of the French style in silk, could be an early form for the man's modern wool suit, though it will have to shed the gold bullion, lace, and many other embellishments before entering the modern closet. Some might argue that the wool suggests a servant's uniform, but the lavishness of the gold contradicts that surmise. Rather, the wool may be an English practicality for cold winters.

French

Man's coat, 1787-1792

Red wool

Purchase, Irene Lewisohn Trust, 1992

(1992.65)

Here is a dashing coat that anticipates
the Macaroni exaggeration that will
characterize menswear in the 1790s. In this
early example, the proportions are already
attenuating; there is a very high turn to the
collar, though not yet to the point of caricature.
This transitional garment is placed then
right on the crucial years of the French
Revolution and is remarkable as an extant
garment from that time.

American

Man's jacket, ca. 1815
Blue checked linen
Purchase, NAMSB Foundation Fund, 1997
(1997.508)

This summer double-breasted cutaway tailcoat
from around 1815 looks fresh enough for
wear today. Its shaping is the counterpart of
womenswear of the period with its high waist,
breadth at the shoulders, and emphasis on the
chest. Faux flap pockets occur at each hip
front, the flaps of which are rounded to a point
in the center. As many have observed,
menswear of this period, just before the Great
Male Renunciation when men spurned any
of the ostensible signs of fashion, was acutely
responsive to womenswear.

Man's suit (jacket, waistcoat, and trousers),
ca. 1829
Navy-blue wool, gray silk faille with floral
pattern, and taupe wool twill
Purchase, NAMSB Foundation Fund and Judith
and Gerson Leiber Fund, 1995 (1995.292a-c)

Also, like the jacket shown above, of the last
decade when men displayed ostentation
in fashion, this unmatched suit is perhaps even
more emphatic in its response to
womenswear. The waist remains high; the
waistcoat may suggest a corset beneath,
and the jacket is now bulky, much like the
vogue in the 1820s for women to wear chunky
velvet, tasseled pelerines or box capes.

Jean Paul Gaultier

Man's suit, spring-summer 1996

Rust and white silk/rayon twill and black wool

Gift of Richard Martin, 1996 (1996.257a,b)

The physique one might wish for is rendered
on the outside of this Gaultier jacket. The facile
effect is that of seeing through clothing, but
the super-effect is that of the idealizing fantasy.
The back works likewise in this theme present
for more than decade in Gaultier's work.
The designer manages to keep the effect fresh
after numerous uses, treating it almost like
a personal leitmotif.

Rei Kawakubo for Comme des Garçons

Man's suit, fall-winter 1994

Gray-green wool crêpe and green wool

Gift of Harold Koda, 1994 (1994.571a,b)

Honoring the tradition of the man's suit while
literally tearing it apart, Kawakubo assaults
the suit, tearing at the lapels into the aftermath
of a ripping, gnashing struggle. The soigné
sartorial catalogue of "suitings" is rendered
raw, in a Levi-Strauss sense, and brutal, basic,
and visible as a fashion process.

Jean Paul Gaultier

Shirt, ca. 1996

Black leather

Gift of Richard Martin, 1996 (1996.386.7)

A sailor's middy is now a torn piece of leather.
Gaultier uses the ripping less as process
the way Kawakubo does and more as narrative.
He turns the crisp sailor of the heroic *H.M.S.
Pinafore*, into the louch Cocteau sailor,
somewhere between a leather bar and
On the Town.

Tom Ford for Gucci

Man's suit (jacket, trousers, and shirt),
fall-winter 1996-1997

Red cotton velvet and blue cotton

Gift of Stephen Cirona, 1999

Tom Ford's designs, derivative of the 1970s,
seize the sensuous indulgence of the lounge
lizard and "Studio 54" era, especially in this
bright velvet suit that seems ready for the
disco floor despite its date of 1996. Ford's
acumen is to make this fashion look new after
an interval of only two decades.

THE AMERICANS

Surprisingly, "The Americans" is the most necessary chapter of this book, as it begins to address a significant gap in the collection. For an American institution, we have only a fair collection of American fashion. Obviously, there are strengths: our early association with the Coty Awards occasioned the deposit of important garments; we have an excellent collection of Claire McCardells, including the primary works of the 1930s wholly absent in another collection that makes great claims to McCardell. But there are serious weaknesses.

In 1993, Harold Koda and I wanted to celebrate our friend Eleanor Lambert's great contribution to fashion in an exhibition we called "Versailles 1973: American Fashion on the World Stage." Harold would not deny that this was the worst of our exhibitions together, including the ten years in both institutions we had served. We had assumed that The Costume Institute had collected important 1970s American fashion. When, too late to withdraw the show, we actually investigated, the depth of the collection was pitiful. After years of gathering Halstons for our Fashion Institute of Technology show "Halston: Absolute Modernism," we knew we had left a far better Halston collection at FIT. We knew the steadfast donors to The Costume Institute had been wearing American designers in the 1960s, 1970s, and 1980s, but they had never found their way to us. We did not even have a Halston Ultrasuede shirtwaist dress, the defining garment of the early 1970s in America. In that case, we turned to an old friend from the earlier Halston exhibition and prevailed upon her to give us the dress we proudly, but sheepishly, show on page 53.

Perforce we began to collect American fashion with zeal. We continue with an enlarged vision to assure that The Costume Institute, which began with a special mission to and from American fashion, advance that charge. We cannot be America's greatest costume collection without an authoritative collection of American costume, which we have made great strides toward establishing. Two exhibitions after the Versailles debacle, "American Ingenuity" (an assessment of American women's sportswear designers, especially in the 1930s and 1940s) and the projected spring 2000 sequel "American Identity" (an examination of the Seventh Avenue acquiescence to Paris in the 1940s and 1950s, resolved only with the emergence of "name" designers in the 1970s, including Bill Blass, Geoffrey Beene, and Halston, clarifying American pragmatism again), stake out a survey of American fashion from the 1930s to the 1970s.

Of course, such a frank admission of our weakest area is intended to elicit donations, as the problem in our American fashion holdings has, in no way, disappeared. Designers who have given us archival collections (major pieces in career survey) have enriched specific areas. But we want the depth of collection we have recently attained for Calvin Klein, Giorgio di Sant'Angelo, Geoffrey Beene, Todd Oldham, and, soon, Ralph Lauren, all through the immense generosity of the designers' (or, in Sant'Angelo's case, Martin Price) deposits of major works, to begin to expand in all categories. The sad truth is that when a collection like this falls behind in one generation of collecting, it takes three generations of solid, retrospective collecting to catch up.

Claire McCardell

Evening gown, late 1940s-early 1950s
Black and red silk plush
Purchase, Polaire Weissman Bequest and Gifts
from various donors, 1997
(1997.511a-d)

With spectacular simplicity, McCardell cut
a bravura swag across the chest with the
elegance of a Madame Grès bodice and
the implicit protocol of a sash or banner.
Applying the same principles of wrapping
that animated her daywear, McCardell also
wrapped for evening, letting the ease of
a plush evening gown define the body with
a gentle boldness. This is an example of
buying an exceptional exhibition-worthy
(it appeared in "American Ingenuity" in
1998) piece by a designer whose work we
already possess in quality and quantity.

Charles James

Wedding gown, 1949
Pale-pink silk satin and ivory silk taffeta
Gift of Jane Love Lee, 1993 (1993.247)

James's wedding gown could, if only it were
a little less seashell-pink, qualify as a John
Singer Sargent pearl, since the nature of its
creation, if a kind of detached and powerful
eroticism, focused in James's case on the
1880s and very likely on Sargent portraiture.
But not even *Madame X.* could command all
the lubricious James signatures seen here: the
low cut of a sweetheart neckline with bare-
shoulder nonchalance, corsetry both restricting
and slightly tumescent as well, a flaring bustle
that Dior might envy, and a center-front
eye-of-the-storm of drapery that only the
seventeenth-century sculptor Giovanni Bernini
could imagine. James was an idealist; few
went to him for wedding gowns for fear
of delays and shenanigans that could result
in the bride ending up at the ceremony as
naked as that emperor with new clothes.

Valentina (Schlee)

Day dress, ca. 1940

Black wool crêpe

Gift of Igor Kamlukin, 1995 (1995.245.3)

The chic dresses of Valentina exemplify cognoscenti high style in New York in the 1940s and 1950s. Her minimalist design was always elegant but never apparent, almost obviating "design." Her discreet black dresses, for example, were always perfect for pictures in the days of black-and-white photography, offering cool, sure graceful frames to the face. While The Costume Institute has long had several Valentina pieces, the collection has been enormously enhanced by a gift of Igor Kamlukin, grand-nephew of the designer. He has also donated Valentina scrapbooks and papers to the Irene Lewisohn Costume Reference Library.

Halston

Shirtwaist dress, 1972

Lavender Ultrasuede

Gift of Faye Robson, 1993 (1993.351a,b)

Fashion had convulsed between maxis and
midis and minis during the 1960s, in what was
undoubtedly an excess of change. Halston is
one of the critical American designers to bring
calm to fashion, quieting the clamorous change
and recognizing consumer resentment. His
Ultrasuede shirtwaist was rational, reasonable
clothing, solving the chaotic clothing problem
for woman. Wrapping, tying, and folding in the
sportswear tradition were all habits of mind for
Halston. He offered a versatile sportswear icon
in a new material, knowing that the shirtwaist
could be interpreted for countless individual
expressions through personal styling.

Rudi Gernreich

Dress, late 1960s
Orange and bright-pink striped knit acrylic
Gift of Richard Martin, 1999

Conceptual designer Rudi Gernreich offered his
clothing as a conceptual art mixed with
publicity-as-art to which he was drawn as
much as Dali or Warhol. He was alert to the art
of his time in a full range: his bathing suits
joined by heavy black tracery resemble the
outlines in the early-twentieth-century paintings
of Georges Rouault or the Op Art works of the
1960s. This trompe l'oeil dress is a single
piece: what looks like a sweater casually
thrown over the shoulders and tied at the front
is actually an integral part of the dress. What is
more American than such a sense of humor?

Calvin Klein

Evening ensemble (halter-top and skirt),
fall 1987
Silver silk charmeuse and black silk
satin-back crêpe
Gift of Calvin Klein, 1998 (1998.508.40a,b)

If there were a way of rating best overall score
in American sportswear, Calvin Klein would
win. Others may surpass him in some
categories, but Klein has mastered the breadth
of sportswear themes. One is separates
dressing, especially for evening, Bill Blass's
forte. If Klein concedes that particular category
to Blass, he concedes nothing else, as this
ensemble that puts casual into a setting of
night and luxury indicates. Perhaps the best
way to evaluate sportswear is not in terms of
one garment but more in terms of the
designer's entire work. Therefore, we are very
grateful that Calvin Klein has worked to give a
large collection of important pieces, often
archive duplicates of their collection, to The
Costume Institute.

Martin Price for Giorgio di Sant'Angelo

Ensemble (bikini-top, hot pants, and jacket), 1992
Gray Persian lamb's wool and gray Mongolian lamb's wool
Gift of Martin F. Price, 1998 (1998.493.5a-c)

Fashion and art are always the first to welcome the outcast into society. Giorgio di Sant'Angelo's ascription of beauty to the gypsy and the prostitute is a significant avowal for the new classless beauty of the 1970s and after. Irony and media have both allowed the transfiguration, but the important and signal statement made by post-1960s fashion is that beauty will not be found in the haughty reiteration of social fashion but in the enlargement of fashion ideas.

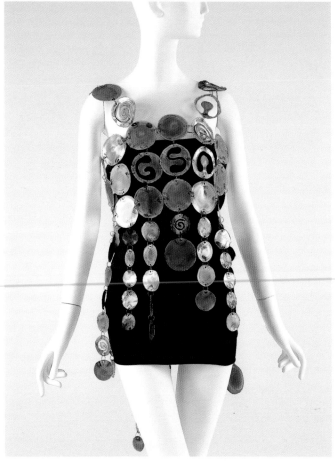

Giorgio di Sant'Angelo

Evening ensemble (overbodice and dress)
(and detail on page 48), 1987
Bronze and black stretch velvet
Gift of Martin F. Price, 1998 (1998.493.538a,b)

Formal wear for Sant'Angelo was as vagabond and exotic as his daywear, thus breaking another fashion convention. His award from the Council of Fashion Designers of America is for his use of stretch material, which brings to fashion the agility necessary for dance and the comfort desirable for active sportswear.

Giorgio di Sant'Angelo

Dress, ca. 1971

Polychrome synthetic chiffon and beige suede

Gift of Martin F. Price, 1998 (1998.493.189)

In one of the great pilgrimages of modern fashion, Giorgio di Sant'Angelo and Diana Vreeland went looking for the gypsy, in pursuit of the more colorful, most authentic, most aboriginal form of manner and dress. That these two unlikely sophisticates came together in this passionate cause is itself romantic; theirs was greater romanticism still; and their discovery in garments of collage and courage and in fearless pages of *Vogue* magazine was yet the greatest romance for style.

Geoffrey Beene

Evening dress, 1991

Black silk crêpe, silver-tone sequins, and black silk point d'esprit

Gift of Anne H. Bass, 1993 (1993.345.12)

Beene lets an evening dress slither over the body with the surety and good grace to profess that beauty is within, just waiting to find the right outline as the dress complements the body. With his craftsman's deftness, Beene creates trustworthy dresses that seem fragile. He has been an exceptionally generous donor and friend, now placing in The Costume Institute fundamental pieces from what has been his archive.

Geoffrey Beene

Evening dress, 1991

Black wool jersey, black silk point d'esprit, and gold-tone sequins

Gift of Anne H. Bass, 1993 (1993.345.11)

The tracing lace provides both closure and aperture in Beene's dress, revealing the body and evoking a distinctive, undulating movement through the little black dress. Beene winds the lace around the body, including front and back, with the ease of Madeleine Vionnet.

Geoffrey Beene

Day suit (bodice, skirt and belt), spring 1995
Navy-blue and white houndstooth check
and navy-blue leather
Gift of Geoffrey Beene, 1997 (1997.97.6a-c)

Using a favorite theme of menswear in a
suitably feminine way, Beene has created an
icon of American sportswear. Of course,
Beene's sportswear is informed by his
traditional training. The result is, like McCardell
or other pioneers, that each gesture is
knowingly made. Beene is in the position of
reinventing sportswear for his generation.

Ralph Lauren

Coat, 1982
Polychrome woven wool
Gift of Ralph Lauren, 1999

No fashion designer has ever written as
spellbinding a history as Lauren has. His epic
of America thrills the spirit; he has rummaged
through the best trading post and found the
most protective, most luxurious, most colorful,
and most self-confident of all the Indian
blankets. Lauren has brilliantly brought
sportswear and narratives together in clothing
that exudes a happy, protected optimism.

THE CONTEMPORARIES

The Costume Institute seeks the Contemporaries. If that sounds like an ad in the Personals, its reckless, desperate implication might be correct. Among traditional museums and certainly within The Metropolitan Museum of Art, the collecting of the contemporary is a vexing, often controversial matter. The policy of The Costume Institute is specific to this curatorial area.

Acknowledging that fashion is an immediate art with elements of utility and design service, The Costume Institute has sought exemption from the Museum's policy of extreme circumspection with respect to the contemporary. On the contrary, The Costume Institute is mandated to deal with the contemporary in a prudent, but mindful, manner. While the Board of Trustees has specifically determined that The Costume Institute may not devote a whole exhibition to one living designer, exhibitions and collections must render appropriate recognition to contemporary fashion. Those policies provide some restrictions: the no-living-designers-shows policy is meant to be exculpatory and may provide some easy excuses. The preponderance of the policy is to allow for and encourage a presence of the contemporary as nowhere else in the Museum.

The subtle and not-so-subtle shifts in exhibitions and collection policy since 1993 have been beneficial, encouraging a careful consideration of every decision involving contemporary fashion. We have not devoted an exhibition to any living designer, yet any visitor to exhibitions can sense design issues of the present that are favored in exhibition inclusions. Arguably, several living designers have already enjoyed the equivalent of a one-person show in the cumulative effect of pieces displayed and display importance within the exhibitions of the 1990s. There is a tonic effect in the placement of the contemporary in a mix of historical periods, the new enlivening the old, the old verifying the new. Without expecting the clothing to enter into conversations with each other, one believes there is a positive effect in possessing both the recent and the historical. As fashion does have, in consumption, the defining aspect of an ephemeral art, we know that we cannot expect to reconstitute the present even a few years from now. A Comme des Garçons lost now could be one lost forever. To forego a Westwood could become a gap in the collection we will never be able to fill. (I think with regret about one specific garment.) In that respect, we are probably further different from other departments with a twentieth-century purview.

Philosopher Gilles Lipovetsky, in lapidary phrase, has coined fashion "the permanent theater of ephemeral metamorphoses." A museum's accustomed policies may wish to bend before such a process, risking that the museum will not possess fashion and an understanding as a process, until it accepts its place in the present. Our rubric is that of "costume" institution, but this institution, located in New York City, was not founded to be a static, detached, or intransigent place. Rather, our progenitor, The Museum of Costume Art, began with a social and cultural mandate to which preservation and exhibition were ancillary. We have not abandoned an involved, passionate, contemporary mission.

Gianni Versace

Evening gown (front and side views), 1998
Black leather, black net, and black beading
and fur
Gift of Gianni Versace, 1999

Worn by Madonna at the "Fire and Ice Ball"
honoring Donatella Versace in Los Angeles in
December 1998, the zipper-gyration evening
gown promises net transparency and/or the
unraveled revelation of the body. Most
importantly, Donatella Versace has taken one
of her brother's signatures—the dress with
see-through plastic or plastic seams—and
expanded it into a more extravagant creation of
her own. The second Versace designer is now
in command of the signature and is taking it in
her own design direction. Gianni Versace was a
generous donor to The Costume Institute; his
sister now continues that tradition.

Ann Demuelemeester

Day ensemble (jacket, pants, shirt, and skirt),
winter 1996-1997
Black wool gabardine, red synthetic knit,
and black synthetic knit
Gift of Ann Demuelemeester, 1998
(1998.513.2a-d)

Among the new designers associated with
Franco-Belgian Deconstructivism,
Demuelemeester is at the forefront. But she is
not an uninvolved artist and she has always
produced accessible fashion, viable in the
fashion world as real clothes. Menswear
elements may be slightly rearranged, but with
congenial good will and with meticulous
tailoring and dressmaking.

Vivienne Westwood

Ensemble (jacket, skirt, dress and bustle)
(front and back views), ca. 1994
Red plaid wool and red plaid cotton/wool blend
Gift of Vivienne Westwood, 1995 (1995.213a-h)

Westwood's gift for historicism realized
either in pastiche or in direct translation is at
work in this outfit, a gift from the designer
after a research visit to The Costume Institute
during which she gave particular attention
to Dior daywear.

Dolce & Gabbana

Evening ensemble (ballgown and shoes), 1996
Copper silk satin
Gift of Susan Sarandon, 1996 (1996.450a,e,f)

Probably the only Academy Awards dress so
far in the collection, this piece was received
for its own merit, its glamorous moment not
forgotten but given little weight in the
judgment process. Associational values
can play a role in certain decisions, though
always a minor one. There is said to be
plans for an Academy Museum in Hollywood
that might accommodate this new category
of notable dresses.

James Galanos

Evening gown, 1980s
Dark-brown, brown and ivory pattern printed on
striped silk satin and plain weave with brown
and ivory beads
Gift of Nancy Reagan, 1995 (1995.71.7a,b)

Our Galanos collection is extensive. By the
1990s, we have become very selective in
accepting new additions. This beautiful dress
would probably have been a strong candidate
for the collection based on its own qualities.
That Mrs. Reagan wore and was donating the
dress probably tipped the balance in its favor.

Catherine Walker

Left: *Ballgown*, 1990
Cream silk organza printed with polychrome rose bouquets
Gift of Mireille Levy, 1998 (1998.218)

Right: *Ballgown*, 1989
White silk chiffon printed with purple tulips and green leaves
Gift of Mrs. Randolph Hearst, 1998 (1998.219)

While The Costume Institute had publicly stated that we would not bid to buy any of Princess Diana's dresses in the 1997 Christie's auction, we said that we might expect to receive one in due course. Due or not, we have received two Catherine Walker ballgowns, both very characteristic of the Princess's style for ceremonial but youthful eveningwear. This is their first showing since their acquisition.

Would we have accepted these dresses if there had been no association with Diana? Probably not. But, while I would not wish The Costume Institute to serve the cult of celebrity, clothing does not entirely lose its social and emotional dimensions simply because it is being considered by a museum. Fashion remains whole and human—always intimate, always feeling—and so must the museum's judgments.

Martin Margiela

Ensemble (study of draping on bust, half dress, and backless vest),
spring-summer 1997
Black silk chiffon and elastic, yellow silk velvet, and tan linen
Gift of Maison Martin Margiela, 1998 (1998.519a,b,d)

Margiela's first presence in a museum exhibition in America was in The Costume Institute's "Infra-Apparel" in 1993. He was in New York for the installation but declined an invitation to the opening. This ensemble, composed of a Stockman dressform as bodice, cloth, and a vest, is a variation on an ensemble we showed in our 1997 show "Wordrobe" to exemplify the conceptual basis of dressmaking. Margiela's paramount concern to return to the raw materials of dress often exchanges finish and finesse for something more akin to process in modern art.

Giorgio Armani

Evening ensemble (bolero and dress),
fall-winter 1995
Yellow silk embroidered with champagne-colored sequins and light-brown beads and yellow silk/Rayon
Gift of Giorgio Armani, 1997 (1997.247.5a,b)

As part of a sizeable gift from the designer that surveys several years of his work, this fine example of Armani eveningwear plays a hot-cool game in which the bolero dazzles against the unpretentious, unadorned dress. Armani's inspiration for the 1930s is apparent here: both thirties movies and fashion (one example is our new Drécoll bolero over a long dress, seen on pages 20-21) featured this elegant styling.

Louis Vuitton by Marc Jacobs

Day ensemble (raincoat and skirt),
fall-winter 1998-1999
Light-gray rubberized cotton and
light-gray organza
Gift of Louis Vuitton, 1999

In his first collection for Louis Vuitton,
American designer Marc Jacobs was unafraid
in making his bold sportswear statement:
proportions, minimalism, and the best fabrics
will make an arresting vision, even with
proven wardrobe basics. Jacobs, a brilliant
interpreter of American popular culture from
smiley faces to Miami hotel towels, has shown
great skill at respecting the circumspect
Vuitton image and tradition.

Christian Lacroix

Evening jacket, fall-winter 1989-1990
Sable fur trimmed with brown braided
chenille and brown silk ribbon
Gift of Mrs. Randolph Hearst, 1997
(1997.486.9)

Evening shorts, fall-winter 1989-1990
Brown silk velvet and rhinestones
Gift of Christian Lacroix, 1998 (1998.495a)

Known primarily for his intense
Postimpressionist and Fauve colors,
Lacroix also creates, as those artists did,
with texture. This fun outfit is about as
tactile as any clothing can possibly be.

Issey Miyake

Dress, spring-summer 1994
Polychrome pleated polyester
Gift of Issey Miyake, 1994 (1994.603.1)

With the vocabulary of pleats that he
introduced in 1990, Miyake has offered wholly
new possibilities for dress. These almost
weightless rolling discs can be compressed or
extended; for packing, they can be flattened.
These "Flying Saucer" dresses are both space
age and as timeless as the paper lanterns
of countless summer parties around the world.
You can push and pull on the dress a good
deal; it goes on over the head; it stays in
motion as you move and/or as other things
around you move. Miyake cherishes the ludic
role of fashion, letting us play with our clothes.

Rei Kawakubo for Comme des Garçons

Dress, spring-summer 1997
Gray and white Nylon gingham
and white Nylon net
Gift of Barneys New York, 1998
(1998.516.1a,b)

In her spring-summer 1997 collection
(one piece from which also appeared in the
"summer" gallery in our 1997 exhibition
"The Four Seasons"), Rei Kawakubo invoked
fashion history with her use of elegant forms
of the torso accentuated by padding. What
confused many observers was body distortion
by restriction or impediment as opposed to
Kawakubo's freedom of body configuration.

Romeo Gigli

Evening suit, ca. 1991

Black silk satin and feathers

Gift of Holly Brubach, 1999 (1999.24.10a,b)

An elegant, but somewhat impractical, dinner suit assumes the position of modern fashion: one can apply one extravagant flourish to a fashion module, but no more. In Yves Saint Laurent's "Bird-of-Paradise" dress for Baroness de Rothschild, it was a sheer T-shirt. Here it is the feathers on a black suit.

THE LIBRARY

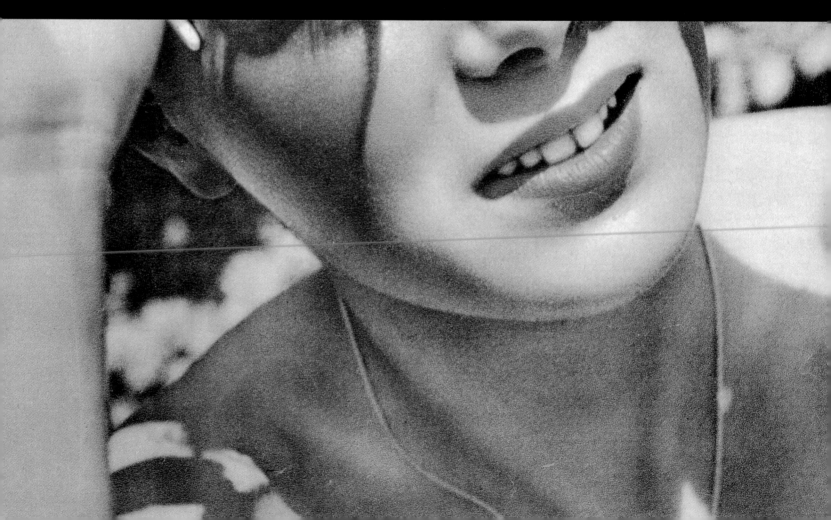

The Irene Lewisohn Costume Reference Library honors in name and in purpose one of the founders of the Museum of Costume Art. The stalwart group who founded the Museum of Costume Art, Inc., in 1937 was primarily interested in scholarship in traditional national costume and resources for the theater. That concern was soon augmented by interest in the history of fashionable clothing as advocated by those and other idealists, who recognized in the 1930s that New York City would become the capital city of the mid-twentieth century. In 1939, with the generous interest of Nelson Rockefeller, the museum visionary, the Museum of Costume Art moved to the International Building in Rockefeller Center with a library.

Inexorably, even as the Museum of Costume Art grew and eventually took up the 1944 offer of The Metropolitan Museum of Art to be housed within the larger museum, the library was a keystone to the Museum of Costume Art's research and service.

Even in dark days when usage dropped and subscriptions lagged, it was understood that costume required its own special bibliography and resources as first identified by the standard volumes of Hiler and Colas, who were in the 1920s and 1930s part of the same historiographic sensibility as the Museum of Costume Art's founders. In some sense, the Irene Lewisohn Library was so much in step with the movement to costume research and bibliography that it is disappointing it is not even more definitive than it is. But these saddest words need not be spoken, for the spirit was clearly earnest and even slightly experimental.

So the spirit remains today. The literature of costume is dispersed in most libraries in classifications that may separate aesthetic principles from social denominations. Moreover, the literature of fashion is equally daunting. The good must be noted as well as the bad in consideration of many cultural phenomena that are inherently so exciting and evanescent. We are at a propitious moment, as the broad, inclusive philosophy of early costume studies accords with the needs of such inquiry today.

Many great donors have assisted The Costume Institute Library in the 1990s, most notably CNN and Elsa Klensch, the late Leo Lerman, Alexander Liberman, and Cora Ginsburg, but those generous donors are only a few among the many. We have created the finest fashion video library in the world, crowned by the 1994 gift of the CNN "Style with Elsa Klensch" collection, selections from which are being presented, for the first time since airing, in this exhibition. We depend upon designers, press offices, and even video producers to keep us up to date in the forms of look-books and videos on contemporary fashion, often up to the day, week, or month, and including contributions from Milan, London, and Paris as well as New York.

Such documents of the present are physically very different from the early fashion plates and photographs that we have also collected. They are equally the record of appearance and of costume. Beginning in the mid-1990s, virtually every exhibition in The Costume Institute has included a book, serial, and document component taken from the Irene Lewisohn Costume Reference Library. *Our New Clothes* would not be a full story without the inclusion of new library resources.

Michael Schmidt

Extra Vermaklyk Lotery-Spel, ca. 1780
Amsterdam: L. Nurbey
Hand-tinted engravings
Irene Lewisohn Costume Reference Library
Gift of Richard Martin, 1998

These engraved cards are from a set portraying
ladies in fashionable headdress and coiffures
from a variety of social classes. They were
used to play a popular Dutch lottery game
of the era, and they correspond to cards with
rhymed sayings having to do with fate, the
second meaning in Dutch of the word "lot."
The cards were bought and sold at prices
based on the class of the woman depicted,
and they provide insight into the iconography
of headdress in eighteenth-century Europe.

Wenceslas Hollar

*Theatrv Muliervm sive Varietas atq.
Differentia Habituum Foeminei Sexus
Diversorum* [sic.] *Europae Nationum;
Hodierno Tempore vulgo in usu
a Wenceslao Hollar etc. Bohemo
Delineatae et Aqua forti aeri*
London: Henry Overton, 1643
Engravings
Irene Lewisohn Costume Reference Library
Gift of Cora Ginsburg, 1997

Shown here are three sheets from the
portfolio of the above title. Anthropology,
history, and travelogue established the need
for analytical description of dress by the
seventeenth century.

Jacques Grasset de Saint-Sauveur

*Costumes des Representans du Peuple
Français: Membres des deux Conseils, de
Directoire Exécutif, Ministres, des Tribunaux,
des Messagers d'Etat, Huissiers, et autres
fonctionnaires Publics.*
Paris: Chez Deroy, 1796
Hand-colored engravings
Irene Lewisohn Costume Reference Library
Purchase, Irene Lewisohn Bequest, 1996

These two engravings are the frontispiece and
a page from the book of the above title.
The new democracy of the period came, as we
know, from Jacques-Louis David's paintings, in
which the sitters dressed in a new way that
sought to establish a new protocol for clothing.

Sinett

Les Cantinières de France
Paris, ca. 1860
Color lithographs
Irene Lewisohn Costume Reference Library
Gift of Richard Martin, 1995

Around 1860, Sinett (a.k.a Sinnett) published
a series of albums that depict the richly
colored uniforms of European troops in a
somewhat romanticized style. Each series
contains twenty-five card-sized color
lithographs. Included are series showing
the English Army, the Bavarian Army,
the Prussian Army, and the Russian Army.
These two examples are from the only
series portraying women in uniform.

Woman in a striped dress, ca. 1865

Two women, 1866

André Adolphe-Eugène Disdéri (1819-1889)

Collection Disdéri: Modes 1860-66
Paris, assembled ca. 1870
Irene Lewisohn Costume Reference Library
Purchase, Irene Lewisohn Trust and Funds
from Various Donors

These two photographs are from a leather-
bound album containing a collection of 176
mounted collodion prints. All are contact
prints of *cartes de visite* portraits, a format
devised by Disdéri. They were collected by
Maurice Levert (1858-1944), secretary to
Prince Victor Napoleon.

Pierre Morgue

Monsieur, cover, October 1921

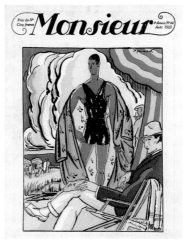

Dignimont

Monsieur, cover, August 1923

*Monsieur: Revue des élégances, des bonnes
manières & de tout ce qui intéresse*
Paris: Éditions Jacques Hébertot Pochoir
Irene Lewisohn Costume Reference Library
Purchase, Irene Lewisohn Bequest, 1995

The men's magazine *Monsieur* ran for six years
(1920-1925). Together with *Gazette du Bon
Ton*, it was a remarkable artistic endeavor and
very influential. Condé Nast and his publishing
and design contemporaries were inspired by
the beautiful quality paper and printing and also
by the superb illustrations and photography.

Page 77: **V. Michal**

Eva, cover, July 1935

Eva: Casopis Vzdelané Zeny
Prague: Melantrich a.s.
Photogravure
Irene Lewisohn Costume Reference Library
Purchase, Irene Lewisohn Bequest, 1996

The subtitle of the magazine *Eva* means
"women's cultural journal." *Eva* occupies an
interesting niche in cosmopolitan prewar
Prague. Avant-garde fashion photography in
thirties Czechoslovakia rivaled that in Paris,
which was nine hours away by automobile.

eva

ČÍSLO 14.

ROČNÍK VII.

CENA 3 Kč

Giorgio di Sant'Angelo *Menswear,* ca. 1980. Watercolor and ink

Above: **Elio**
Man in a Blue Suit, ca. 1932
Gouache
The Harry Simons Archive
Irene Lewisohn Costume Reference Library
Gift of Lisa Kaminsky, 1999

Page 78: **Anonymous**
Two Men in Interior, 1939
Pencil, ink, and ink wash
The Harry Simons Archive
Irene Lewisohn Costume Reference Library
Gift of Lisa Kaminsky, 1999

These two sheets are in the archive of
Harry Simons (1878-1967), menswear
tailoring pioneer, who published trade
magazines, patterns, books, and pamphlets,
and invented machines for pattern making,
pattern storage, and measuring. His
granddaughter donated the archive to the
Irene Lewisohn Costume Reference Library.

Giorgio di Sant'Angelo
Showtime (Jacquard Knits), 1976. Ink

Giorgio di Sant'Angelo
The Romantic Melodies, 1977. Pencil

The Giorgio di Sant'Angelo Archive
Irene Lewisohn Costume Reference Library
Gift of Martin Price, 1998

These three drawings are part of the most
comprehensive design archive in the library's
history, the Martin Price donation, which
complements the donation of clothing made to
The Costume Institute. Among the archives
riches are: Sant'Angelo's sketchbooks from the
1970s and 1980s; photographs of his designs
by Franco Rubartelli, Robert Mappelthorpe,
and others; press notebooks for collections
from the late 1960s to 1990; design sketches
in a myriad of styles and media; fully-realized
framed design sketches from the 1960s and
1970s; fine arts projects by Sant'Angelo,
including textiles and paintings; press kits and
advertising materials from most of the
collections; and programs from performers'
fashions he designed, Lena Horne and Mick
Jagger included.

ACKNOWLEDGMENTS

As I accepted Philippe de Montebello's suggestion of a recent acquisitions show, proclaiming "Fine, what about spring 1999," I was imagining the galleries in accordance with these themes, the time span of the 1990s, and even this book. The title came a few days later, circuitously, through Hans Christian Andersen, but even then in a like spirit. For *Our New Clothes* is, in its way, a fairy tale. The assembly, preservation, documentation, presentation, and interpretation of The Costume Institute is a delight, an enchantment, a wonder. It's not a job; it's a dream.

But fairy tales have villains and witches. This one has no such characters. It certainly has the benevolent fairy godmothers who have given us the treasures we assemble here and the many that surpass the finite space of this book and exhibition but contribute immeasurably to the collection of The Costume Institute. We thank them all. The pleasure of working as part of such a talented, gifted team at The Costume Institute is blissful. Specifically, with respect to *Our New Clothes*, I thank: Amy Beil, Anne Byrd, Edith de Montebello, Deirdre Donohue, Michael Downer, Minda Drazin, Lisa Faibish, Ellen Fisher, Rochelle Friedman, Elizabeth Gaston, Angelica Glass, Dorothy Hanenberg, Barbara Havranek, Rebecca Hoffman, Stéphane Houy-Towner, Alexandra Kowalski, Marianna Kuhn, Wade La Boissonniere, Marilyn Lawrence, Emily Martin, Bonnie Rosenblum, Birdie Schklowsky, Rose Simon, and Judith Sommer. You are dreamy to me, my dream team. Most special to *Our New Clothes* are those who animate the garments. Chris Paulocik's loving and analytical care in conservation and Jennifer Kibel's acumen and style in dressing are evident in each photograph and in the exhibition. Behind the camera, Karin Willis has become all but a dressmaker through her keen eye.

Fairy tales come in large-scale tomes, but none could be more handsome or finer than this little book is to me, thanks to the marvelous friendship and princely spirit of John P. O'Neill and the aid of Barbara Cavaliere, whose telepathic editing has always seemed magic. Takaaki Matsumoto (of Matsumoto Incorporated) is Merlin: he conjures and composes an elegant book from myriad pieces; he is ably assisted by Branwen Jones and Takuyo Takahashi. After some dozen years of our work together, I am still amazed by his graphic prestidigitation. I want to express my deep appreciation to those who have given special assistance to *Our New Clothes*: Simon Doonan, David New, and Jason Weisenfeld of Barneys New York; Cora Ginsburg and Titi Halle of Cora Ginsburg; Martin Kamer; Martin Price; Patrizia Cucco, Marcus Ebner, Ed Filipowski of Gianni Versace. At The Metropolitan Museum of Art, I thank Richard R. Morsches, Linda Sylling, Barbara Weinberg, Martin Bansbach, Michael Langley, Sue Koch, and Bernice Kwok-Gabel.

Every tale needs fairy godmothers and gentle guides: Kitty Benton, Barbara Brickman, Julie Duer, Nancy DuPuy, Eileen Ekstract, Susan Furlaud, Betsy Kallop, Susan Lauren, Butzi Moffit, Victoria Munroe, Wendy Nolan, Pat Peterson, Christine Petschek, Dee Schaeffer, Nancy Silbert, and D. J. White are mine. They are loved and esteemed.

Fairy tale is superseded by truth: the world's finest collection of costume has made enormous strides in the past ten years to remain peerless, ever better and more effective. That is the truth: I could only be dreaming to have the privilege to declare so.

Richard Martin
Curator, The Costume Institute,
The Metropolitan Museum of Art